THE
CHALDÆAN
ORACLES

G. R. S. MEAD

British Library Cataloguing in Publication Data

A catalogue record for this book is available from the British
Library

ISBN-13: 978-1-908388-26-1

Printed and bound in Great Britain by Lightning Souce UK
Ltd., 6 Precedent Drive, Rooksley, Milton Keynes MK13 8PR.

Cover Illustration: *Hecate* (detail). William Blake (c.1795)

ECHOES FROM THE GNOSIS

Under this general title is now being published a series of small volumes, drawn from, or based upon, the mystic, theosophic and gnostic writings of the ancients, so as to make more easily audible for the ever-widening circle of those who love such things, some echoes of the mystic experiences and initiatory lore of their spiritual ancestry. There are many who love the life of the spirit, and who long for the light of gnostic illumination, but who are not sufficiently equipped to study the writings of the ancients at first hand, or to follow unaided the labours of scholars. These little volumes are therefore intended to serve as introduction to the study of the more difficult literature of the subject; and it is hoped that at the same time they may become for some, who have, as yet, not even heard of the Gnosis, stepping-stones to higher things.

G. R. S. M.

CONTENTS.

BIBLIOGRAPHY

K. = Kroll (G.), De Oraculis Chaldaicis; in Breslauer philologische Abhandlungen, Bd. vii., Hft. i. (Breslau; 1894).

C. = Cory (I. P.), Ancient Fragments (London; 2nd ed., 1832), pp. 239-280. The first and third editions do not contain the text of our Oracles.

F. = Mead (G. R. S.), Fragments of a Faith Forgotten (London; 2nd. ed., 1906).

H. = Mead (G. R. S.), Thrice Greatest Hermes (London; 1906).

THE
CHALDÆAN
ORACLES

INTRODUCTION

The Chaldæan Oracles (Lógia, Oracula, Responsa) are a product of Hellenistic (and more precisely Alexandrian) syncretism.

The Alexandrian religio-philosophy proper was a blend of Orphic, Pythagoræan, Platonic, and Stoic elements, and constituted the theology of the learned in the great city which had gradually, from the third century B.C., made herself the centre of Hellenic culture.

In her intimate contact with the Orient, the mind of Greece freely united with the mysterious and enthusiastic cults and wisdom-traditions of the other nations, and became very industrious in "philosophizing" their mythology, theosophy and gnosis, their oracular utterances, symbolic apocalypses and initiatory lore.

The two nations that made the deepest impression on the Greek thinkers were Egypt and Chaldæa; these they regarded as the possessors of the most ancient wisdom-traditions.

How Hellenism philosophized the ancient wisdom of Egypt, we have already shown at great length in our volumes on Thrice-greatest Hermes. The Chaldæan Oracles are a parallel endeavour, on a smaller scale, to philosophize the wisdom of Chaldæa. In the Trismegistic writings, moreover, we had to deal with a series of prose treatises, whereas in our Oracles we are to treat of the fragments of a single mystery-poem, which may with advantage be compared with the cycle of Jewish and Christian pseudepigraphic poems known as the Sibylline Oracles.

The Great Library of Alexandria contained a valuable collection of MSS. of what we may term the then "Sacred Books of the East" in their original tongues. Many of these were translated, and among them the "Books of the Chaldæans." Thus Zosimus, the early alchemist, and a member of one of the later Trismegistic communities, writes, somewhere at the end of the third century A. D.:

"The Chaldæans and Parthians and Medes and Hebrews call him [the First Man] Adam, which is by interpretation virgin Earth, and blood-red Earth, and fiery Earth, and fleshly Earth.

"And these indications were found in the book-collections of the Ptolemies, which they stored away in every temple, and especially in the Serapeum" (H., iii., 277).

The term Chaldæan is, of course, vague, and scientifically inaccurate. Chaldæan is a Greek synonym for Babylonian, and is the way they transliterated the Assyrian name Kaldâ . The land of the Kaldâ proper lay S.E. of Babylonia proper on what was then the sea-coast. As the Encyclopædia Biblica informs us:

"The Chaldæans not only furnished an early dynasty of Babylon, but also were incessantly pressing into Babylonia; and, despite their repeated defeats by Assyria, they gradually gained the upper hand there. The founder of the New Babylonian Kingdom, Nabopolassar (circa 626 B.C.), was a Chaldæan, and from that time Chaldæa meant Babylonia....

"We find 'Chaldæans' used in Daniel, as a name for a caste of wise men. As Chaldæan meant Babylonian in the wider sense of a member of the dominant race in the times of the new Babylonian Empire, so after the Persian conquest it seems to have connoted the Babylonian literati and became a synonym of soothsayer and astrologer. In this sense it passed into classical writers."

We shall, however, see from the fragments of our poem that some of the Chaldæi were something more than soothsayers and astrologers.

As to our sources; the disjecta membra of this lost mystery-poem are chiefly found in the books and commentaries of the Platonici - that is, of the Later Platonic school. In addition to this there are extant five treatises of the Byzantine period, dealing directly with the doctrines of the "Chaldæan philosophy": five chapters of a book of Proclus, three treatises of Psellus (eleventh century), and a letter of a contemporary letter-writer, following on Psellus.

But by far the greatest number of our fragments is found in the books of the Later Platonic philosophers, who from the time of Porphyry (fl. c. 250-300) - and, therefore, we may conclude from that of Plotinus, the corypheus of the school - held these Oracles in the highest estimation. Almost without a break, the succession of the Chain praise and comment elaborately on them, from Porphyry onwards - Iamblichus, Julian the Emperor, Synesius, Syrianus, Proclus, Hierocles - till the last group who flourished in the first half of the sixth century, when Simplicius, Damascius and Olympiodorus were still busy with the philosophy of our Oracles.

Some of them - Porphyry, Iamblichus and Proclus - wrote elaborate treatises on the subject; Syrianus wrote a "symphony" of Orpheus, Pythagoras and Plato with reference to and in explanation of the Oracles; while Hierocles, in his treatise On Providence, endeavoured to bring the doctrine of the Oracles into "symphony" with the dogmas of the Theurgists and the philosophy of Plato. All these books are, unfortunately, lost, and we have to be content with the scattered, though numerous, references, with occasional quotations, in such of their other works as have been preserved to us.

In this brief introduction it would take too long to discuss the "literature" of the Oracles; and indeed this is all the more unnecessary as until the work of Kroll appeared, the subject had never been treated scientifically. Prior to Kroll it had been, more or less, generally held that the Oracles were a collection of sayings deriving immediately from the Chaldæan wisdom, and even by some as direct translations or paraphrases from a Chaldæan original.

This was the general impression made by the vagueness with which the Later Platonic commentators introduced their authority; as, for instance: The Chaldæan Oracles, the Chaldæans, the Assyrians, the Foreigners (lit., Barbarians or Natives), the God-transmitted Wisdom, or Mystagogy handed on by the Gods; and, generally, simply: The Oracles, the Oracle, the Gods, or one of the Gods.

Kroll has been the first to establish that for all this there was but a single authority - namely, a poem in hexameter verse, in the conventional style of Greek Oracular utterances, as is the case with the Sibyllines and Homeric centones.

The fragments of this poem have, for the most part, been preserved to us by being embedded in a refined stratum of elaborate commentary, in which the simple forms of the poetical imagery and the symbolic expressions of the original have been blended with the subtleties of a highly developed and abstract systematization, which is for the most part foreign to the enthusiastic and vital spirit of the mystic utterances of the poem.

To understand the doctrines of the original poem, we must recover the fragments that remain, and piece them together as best we can under general and natural headings; we must not, as has previously been done, content ourselves with reading them through the eyes of the philosophers of the Later Platonic School, whose one pre-occupation was not only to make a "harmony" or "symphony" between Orpheus, Pythagoras, Plato and the Oracles, but also to wrest the latter into accommodation with their own elaborations of Platonic and Plotinian doctrine.

When we have done this, we shall have before us the remains of a mystery-poem, addressed to "initiates," and evidently forming part of the inner instruction of a School or Community; but even so we shall not have the clear original, for there are several interpolations, which have crept in with the tradition of the text from hand to hand of many scribes.

What is the date of this original poem? It was known to Porphyry. Now Porphyry (Malek) was a Semite by birth and knew Hebrew; he may also have known "Chaldæan." At any rate we know he was a good scholar and had good critical ability, and that he was at pains to sift out "genuine" from spurious "Oracles," thus showing that there were many Oracles circulating in his day. The genuine ones he collected in his lost work entitled, On the Philosophy of the Oracles, and among them was our poem.

Kroll places this poem at the end of the second century or the beginning of the third, chiefly because it breathes the spirit of a "saving cult," and such cults, he believes, did not come into general prominence till the days of Marcus Aurelius (imp. 161-180). But saving cults had been a common-place of the East and in Alexandria for centuries, and this, therefore, does not seem to me to afford us any indication of date.

The two Julians, father and son, moreover, the former of whom Suidas calls a "Chaldæan philosopher," and the latter "the Theurgist," adding that the son flourished under Marcus Aurelius, will hardly help us in this connection; for the father wrote a book On Daimones only, and, though the son wrote works on theurgy and also on the oracles of theurgy and the "secrets of this science," Porphyry did not associate him with our Oracles, for he devoted a separate book of commentaries (now lost) to "The Doctrines of Julian the Chaldæan," while Proclus and Damascius dissociate this Julian from our Oracles, by quoting him separately under the title "The Theurgist" (K. 71).

Porphyry evidently considered our Oracles as old, but how old? To this we can give no precise answer. The problem is the same as that which confronts us in both the Trismegistic and

Sibylline literature, which can be pushed back in an unbroken line to the early years of the Ptolemaic period. We are, therefore, justified in saying that our poem may as easily be placed in the first as in the second century.

It remains only to be remarked that, as might very well be expected with such scattered shreds and fragments of highly poetical imagery and symbolic and mystical poetry, the task of translation is often very arduous, all the more so owing to the absence of truly critical texts of the documents from which they are recovered. Kroll has supplied us with an excellent apparatus and many emendations of the tradition of the printed texts; but until the extant works of the Later Platonic School are critically edited from the MSS. (as has been done only in a few instances) a truly critical text of our Oracle-fragments is out of the question. Kroll has printed all the texts, both of the fragments and of the contexts, in the ancient authors, where they are found, in his indispensable treatise in Latin on the subject, but, as is usual with the work of specialists, he does not translate a single line. With these brief remarks we now present the reader with a translation and comments on the fragments of what might be called "The Gnosis of the Fire."

FRAGMENTS
AND
COMMENTS

THE SUPREME PRINCIPLE.

In the extant fragments of our Oracle-poem the Supreme Principle is characterized simply as Father, or Mind, or Mind of the Father, or again as Fire.

Psellus, however, in his commentary, declares that the Oracles hymned the Source of all as the One and Good (K. 10); and there can be little doubt that in the circle of our poet, the Deity was either regarded as the "One and All" - according to the grand formula of Heraclitus (fl. 500 B.C.), who had probably to some extent already "philosophized" the intuitions and symbols of a Mago-Chaldæan tradition - or, as with so many Gnostic schools of the time, was conceived of as the Ineffable.

Cory, in his collection of Oracle-fragments, includes (C. I) a definition of the Supreme which Eusebius attributed to the "Persian Zoroaster." This may very well have been derived from some Hellenistic document influenced by the "Books of the Chaldæans," or "Books of the Medes," and may, therefore, be considered as generally consonant with the basic doctrine of our Oracles. As, however, Kroll rightly omits this, we append it in illustration only.

"He is the First, indestructible, eternal, ingenerable, impartible, entirely unlike aught else, Disposer of all beauty, unbribable, of all the good the Best, of all the wisest the Most Wise; the Father of good-rule and righteousness is He as well, self-taught, and natural, perfect, and wise, the sole Discoverer of sacred nature-lore."

THE END OF UNDERSTANDING.

If, however, we have no excerpt bearing directly on the Summum Mysterium, we have enough, and more than enough, to support us in our conjecture that it was conceived of in our Oracles as being itself beyond all words, in a fragment of eleven lines which sets forth the supreme end of contemplation as follows:

Yea, there is That which is the End-of-   K. II.
understanding, the That which   C. 163.
thou must understand with flower of mind.

For should'st thou turn thy mind inwards   167
on It, and understand It as understanding
"something," thou shalt not understand It.

For that there is a power of [the mind's]   61
prime that shineth forth in all directions,
flashing with intellectual rays [lit., sectors].   62

Yet, in good sooth, thou should'st not [strive]
with vehemence [to] understand that End-of-
understanding, nor even with the wide-
extended flame of wide-extended mind that   166
measures all things - except that End-of-
understanding [only].

Indeed there is no need of strain in
understanding This; but thou should'st
have the vision of thy soul in purity, turned
from aught else, so as to make thy mind,
empty [of all things else], attentive to that
End, in order that thou mayest learn that
End-of-understanding; for It subsists beyond
the mind.

The "That which is the End-of-understanding" is generally rendered the Intelligible. But to no' tón, for the Gnostic of this tradition, in this connection signifies the Self-creative Mind, that is, the Mind that creates its own understanding.

It is both the simultaneous beginning and end, or cause and result of itself; and thus is the end or goal of all understanding. It has, therefore, to be distinguished from all formal modes of intellection; the normal mind that is conditioned by the opposites, subject and object, cannot grasp it. So long as we conceive it as object, as other than ourselves, as though we are "understanding 'something,'" so long are we without it. It must be contemplated with the "flower of mind," by mind in its "prime," that is, at the moment of blossoming of the growing mind, which rays within and without in intellectual brilliance, both penetrating its own depths and becoming one with them.

"Flower of mind," however, is not the fruit or jewels of mind, though it is a power of fiery mind, for flowers are on the sun-side of things. To understand "with flower of mind" thus seems to suggest to catch, like petals, in a cup-like way, with the *krat' res* or deeps of mind, the true fiery intelligence of the Great Mind, as flowers catch the sun-rays, and by means of them to bring to birth within oneself the fruit or jewels of the Mind, which are of the nature of immediate or spiritual understanding, that is to say, the greater mind-senses, or powers of understanding.

The fragment seems to be an instruction in a method of initiating the mind in understanding or true gnosis - a very subtle process. It is not to be expected that the normal, formal, partial mind can seize a complete idea, a fullness, as it erroneously imagines it does in the region of form; in the living intelligible "spheres" there are no such limited ideas defined by form or outline; they are measureless.

In this symbolism flame and flower are much the same; flame of mind and flower of mind suggest the same happening in the "mineral" and "vegetable" kingdoms of the mind-realms. The mind has to grow of itself towards its sun. Most men's minds are at best smouldering fire; they require a "breath" of the Great Breath to make them burst into flame, and so extend themselves, or possess themselves of new re-generative power. Most men's minds, or persons, are unripe plants; we have not yet brought ourselves to the blossoming point. This is achieved only by Heat from the Sun. A blossoming person may be said to be one who is beginning to know how to form fruit and re-generate himself.

In this vital exercise of inner growth there must be no formal thinking. The personal mind must be made empty or void of all preconceptions, but at the same time become keenly attentive, transformed into pure sense, or capacity for greater sensations. The soul must be in a searching frame of mind, searching not enquiring, that is to say synthetic not analytic. Enquiry suggests penetrating into a thing with the personal mind; while searching denotes embracing and seizing ideas, "eating" or "digesting" or "absorbing" them, so to say; getting all round them and making them one's own, surrounding them - it is no longer a question of separated subject and object as with the personal and analyzing mind.

MYSTIC UNION

The whole instruction might be termed a method of yoga or mystic union (unio mystica) of the spiritual or kingly mind, the mind that rules itself - *raja-yoga,* the royal art proper. But there must be no "vehemence" (no "fierce impetuosity," to use a phrase of Patañjali's in his *Yoga-sã tra*) in one direction only; there must be expansion in every direction within and without in stillness.

The "vision" of the soul is, literally, the "eye" of the soul. The mind must be emptied of every object, so that it may receive the fullness. It becomes the "pure eye," the æon, all-eye; not, however, to perceive anything other than itself, but to understand the nature of understanding - namely, that it transcends all distinctions of subject and object.

And yet though the Reality may be said to be "beyond the mind," or "without it," it is really not so. It may very well be said to be beyond or transcend the personal or formal mind, or mind in separation, for that is the mind that separates; but the Intelligible and the Mind-in-itself are really one. As one of the fragments says:

K. II.   *For Mind is not without the That-which-*
           makes-it-Mind; and That-which-is-the-
           End-of-Mind doth not subsist apart
C. 43.44   *from Mind.*

Both these hyphened terms represent the same word in Greek, usually rendered the Intelligible. The Oracle might thus be made to run: "For Intellect is not without the Intelligible, and the Intelligible subsists not apart from Intellect." But this makes τὸ νοητόν the object only of understanding; whereas it is neither subject nor object, but both.

THE ONE DESIRABLE

The Father is the Source of all sources and the End of all ends; He is the One Desirable, Perfect and Benignant, the Good, the Summum Bonum, as we learn from the following three disconnected fragments.

K. 15.   *For from the Paternal Source naught*
C. 9.   *that is imperfect spins [or wheels].*

The soul must have measure, rhythm, and perfection, to spin, circulate or throb with this Divine Principle.

K. 15.   *The Father doth not sow fear, but pours*
C. 10.   *forth persuasion.*

The Father controls from within and not from without; controls by being, by living within, and not by constraining.

K. 15.   *Not knowing that God is wholly Good.*
C. 184.   *O wretched slaves, be sober!*

Compare with this the address of the preacher inserted in the Trismegistic "Man-Shepherd" treatise (H., ii. 17):

"O ye people, earth-born folk, ye who have given yourselves to drunkenness and sleep and ignorance of God, be sober now!"

And also the Oracle quoted as follows:

The soul of men shall press God closely to itself,
with naught subject to death in it; [but now] it is
all drunk, for it doth glory in the Harmony [that
is, the Sublunary or Fate Spheres] beneath whose
sway the mortal frame exists.

THE DIVINE TRIAD

How the Divine Simplicity conditions its self-revelation no fragment tells us. But in spite of Kroll's scepticism I believe the Later Platonic commentators were not wrong when they sought for it in the riddle of the triad or trinity.

The doctrine of the Oracles as to the Self-conditioning of the Supreme Monad may, however, perhaps, be recovered from the passage of the Simonian *Great Announcement* quoted in our last little volume (pp. 40 ff). This striking exposition of the Gnosis was "philosophized" upon a Mago-Chaldæan background, and that, too, at a date at least contemporaneous with the very origins of Christianity, as is now, I think,

demonstrated with high probability (H., i. 184). The passage is so important that it deserves re-quotation; but as it is so easily accessible, it may be sufficient simply to refer the interested reader to it.

Centuries before Proclus this tripartite or triadic dogma was known to the Greeks as pre-eminently Assyrian, that is Syrian or Chaldæan. Thus Hippolytus, commenting on the Naassene Document, in which the references to the Initiatory Rites are pre-Christian, writes:

"And first of all, in considering the triple division of Man [the Monad or Logos], they [the Naassenes] fly for help to the Initiations of the Assyrians; for the Assyrians were the first to consider the Soul triple and yet one" (H., i. 151).

In the same Document the early Jewish commentator, who was in all probability a contemporary of Philo's in the earliest years of the Christian era, gives the first words of a mystery-hymn which run: "*From Thee* is Father and *Through*

Thee Mother" (ibid., 146); and, it might be added: "To Thee is Son." This represents the values of the three "Great Names" on the Path of Return; but in the Way of Descent, that is of cosmogenesis, or world-shaping, their values would differ. Curiously enough one of our Oracles reads:

For Power is With Him, *but Mind* From Him.

Power always represents the Mother-side (the Many), the Spouse of Deity (the Mind, the One), and Son is the Result, the "From Him" - the Mind in manifestation. Hence we read of the Father, or Mind Proper, as becoming unmanifested or withdrawn, or hidden, after giving the First Impulse to Himself.

The Father withdrew Himself, yet shut not up His own peculiar Fire within His Gnostic Power.

"His own peculiar Fire" seems to mean that which characterizes the One Mystery as Father, or creative. He withdrew Himself into Silence and Darkness, but left His Fire, or Fiery Mind, to operate the whole creation. May not this throw some light on the meaning of the obscure mystery-hymn at the end of the Christian Gnostic Second Book of Ieou (Carl Schmidt, Gnost. Schrift., p. 187)?

"I praise Thee . . .; for Thou hast drawn Thyself into Thyself altogether in Truth, till Thou hast set free the space of this Little Idea (? the manifested cosmos]; yet hast Thou not withdrawn Thyself."

GOD-NURTURING SILENCE

In the first passage from the Simonian *Great Announcement,*
to which we have referred above (p. 31), the Great Power
of the Father is called Incomprehensible Silence, and, as
is well known, Silence (Sig') was, in a number of systems
of the Christianized Gnosis, the Syzygy, or Co-partner, or
Complement, of the Ineffable. Among the Pythagoræans
and Trismegistic Gnostics also Silence was the condition of
Wisdom.

Though there is no verse of our Oracle-poem preserved
which sets this forth, there are phrases quoted by Proclus (K.
16) which speak of the Paternal Silence. It is the Divine "*Calm,*"
the "*Silence, Nurturer of the Divine*"; it is the unsurpassable
unity of the Father, the that concerning which words fail; the
mind must be silenced to know it - that is, to "accord with" it
(K. 16, C. 12, 5).

Proclus in all probability had our Oracles in mind when he
wrote (C. 12):

"For such is the Mind in that state, energizing prior to
energizing [in the sensible world, in that it had in no way
emanated, but rested in the Father's Depth [i.e., its own
Depth], and in the Sacred Shrine, held in the Arms of Silence,
'*Nurturer of the Divine.*'"

Silence is known through mind alone. While things are
objective to one, while we are taught or told *about* things, they
cannot be real. The Great Silence on the mind-side of things
corresponds with the Great Sea on the matter-side of things;
the latter is active, the former inactive; and the only way to

28

attain wisdom, which is other than knowledge, is to "re-create" or re-generate oneself. Man only "knows" God by getting to this Silence, in which naught but the creative words of true Power are heard. He then no longer conceives formal ideas in his mind, but utters living ideas in all his acts - thoughts, words and deeds.

The Fatherhood is equated by Proclus (K. 13) with Essence (*ousía*), or Subsistence (*hyparxis*); the Motherhood with Life, or Power (*dynamis*); and the Sonship with Operation or Actuality (*enérgeia*). These philosophical terms are, of course, not the names used in the Oracles, which preferred more graphic, symbolic and poetical expressions.

THE HOLY FIRE

Thus Mind "in potentiality" is the "Hidden Fire" of Simon the Magian (who doubtless knew of the "Books of the Chaldæans"), and the "Manifested Fire" was the Mind "in operation" or Formative Mind. As *The Great Announcement* of the Simonian tradition has it (Hipp., Ref., vi. 9-11):

"The hidden aspects of the Fire are concealed in the manifest, and the manifest produced in the hidden. . . .

"And the manifested side of the Fire has all things in itself which a man can perceive of things visible, or which he unconsciously fails to perceive; whereas the hidden side is every thing which one can conceive as intelligible, or which a man fails to conceive."

And so in our Oracles, as with Simon, and with Heraclitus, who called it "Ever-living Fire," the greatest symbol of the Power of Deity was called "*Holy Fire*", as Proclus tells us (K. 13). This Fire was both intelligible and immaterial and sensible and material, according to the point of view from which it was regarded.

MIND OF MIND

The fiery self-creative Energy of the Father is regarded as intelligible; that is, as determined by the vital potencies of Mind alone. Here all is "in potentiality" or hidden from the senses; it is the truly "occult world." The sensible, or manifested, universe comes into existence by the demiurgic, or formative, or shaping Energy of the Mind, which now, as Architect of matter, is called Mind of Mind, or Mind Son of Mind, as we have Man Son of Man in the Christianized Chaldæan Gnosis. This is set forth in the following lines:

K. 13.   *For He [the Father] doth not in-lock*
          His Fire transcendent, the Primal Fire,
          His Power, into Matter by means of
          works, but by energy of Mind.
C. 22.   *For it is Mind of Mind who is the*
          Architect of this [the manifested] fiery
          world.

"Works" seem here to mean activities, objects, creatures - separation. This Father, who is wholly beyond the Sea of Matter, does not shut up His Power into Matter by in-locking it in bodies, or works, or separate objects, but energizes by means of some mysterious abstract and infinite penetration - thus laying down as it were the foundations of root-form, the ground-plan so to speak, the nexus of the first Limit; this makes Matter to assume the first beginnings of Mass. As soon as the Father, or Mind of all minds, has made this frame-work or net-work of Fire, Mind of Mind is born; and this Mind is the Fiery Cosmic Mind, which by contacting Matter in its first essential nature generates the beginnings of the World-Body and of all bodies. This is the work of Mind of Mind.

So also we find the Supreme addressing Hermes in "The Virgin of the World" treatise as:

"Soul of My Soul, and Holy Mind of My own Mind" (H., iii. 104).

And again in another Trismegistic fragment we read:

"There was One Gnostic Light alone - nay, Light transcending Gnostic Light. He is for ever Mind of Mind who makes that Light to shine" (H., iii. 257).

For as our Oracles have it:

K. 14.   *The Father out-perfected all, and gave*
          them over to His second Mind,
C. 13.   *whom ye, all nations of mankind, sing*
          of as first.

Intelligible Fire has the essence of all things for its "sparks" or "atoms."

"Out-perfected" seems to mean that the Father of Himself is the Complement or Fulfilment of each separate thing. In a certain mystic sense, there are never more than two things in the universe - namely, any one thing which one may choose to think of, and its complement, the rest of the All; and that completion of every imperfection is God.

The contention of the Gnostics was that the nations worshipped the Demiurgic or Fabricative Power of the Deity as His most transcendent mystery; this, they contended, was really a secondary mode of the Divine Power as compared with the mystery of the ineffable Self-determination of the Supreme.

A volume might be written on the subject, with innumerable quotations from Jewish and Christian Gnostics, from Philo and the Trismegistic writers, and from early Orientalist Platonists such as Numenius. The Father, as Absolute Mind, or Paramatman, perfects all things; but when we distinguish Spirit and Matter, when we regard the mystery from our state of duality, and imagine Matter as set over against Spirit, then the administration of Matter is said to be entrusted to Mind in operation in space and time; and this was called Mind of Mind, Mind Son of Mind, or Man Son of Man.

THE MONAD AND DYAD

This Mind of Mind is conceived as dual, as containing the idea of the Dyad, in contrast with the Paternal Mind which is the Monad - both terms of the Pythagoræan *mathesis* or *gnosis*. His duality consists in His having power over both the intelligible and sensible universe. This is set forth in our Oracles as follows:

K. 14.   The Dyad hath His seat with Him [the
                    Father]; for He hath both - [both power]
C. 27.   to master things intelligible [or ideal],
                    and also to induce the sense of feeling
                    in the world [of form].

Nevertheless, there are not two Gods, but one; not two Minds, but one; not two Fires, but one; for:

K. 15.   All things have for their Father the One
C. 13.   Fire.

    The Father is thus called the Paternal Monad.

K. 15.   He is the all-embracing [lit., wide-
C. 26.   stretching] Monad who begets the Two.

THE ONE BODY OF ALL THINGS

In connection with this verse we may take the following two verses of very obscure reading:

From both of these [the Monad and Dyad] there flows the Body of the Three, first yet not first; for it is not by it that things intelligible are measured.

This appears to mean that, for the sensible universe, the Body of the Triad - that is, the Mother-substance - comes first as being the container of all things sensible; it is not, however, the measurer of things intelligible or ideal. It is first as Body, or the First or Primal Body, but Mind is prior to it.

ONCE BEYOND AND TWICE BEYOND

The Three Persons of the Supernal Triad were also called in the Oracles by the names Once Beyond, Twice Beyond and Hecate ; when so called they seem to have been regarded by the commentators as either simply synonyms of the three Great Names, or else as in some way the self-reflection of the Primal Triad, or as the Primal Triad mirrored in itself, that is in the One Body of all things.

It is difficult to say what is the precise meaning of the mystery-names Once Beyond and Twice Beyond. If we take them as designations of the self-reflected Triad, it may be that Once Beyond was so called because it was regarded as Beyond, not in the sense of transcending, but as beyond the threshold, so to say, of the pure spiritual state, or, in other words, as raying forth into manifestation; and so also with Twice Beyond. They paralleled the first and second Minds of the Primal Unity.

Hecate seems to have been the best equivalent our Greek mystics could find in the Hellenic pantheon for the mysterious and awe-inspiring Primal Mother or Great Mother of Oriental mystagogy.

This reflected Trinity seems to have been regarded as the Three-in-one of the Second Mind. The Later Platonist commentators seem to have in general equated these names with their Kronos, Zeus and Rhea; while an anonymous commentator earlier than Proclus tells us that Once Beyond is the Paternal Mind of all cosmic intellection; Hecate is the ineffable Power of this Mind and fills all things with intellectual light, but apparently does not enter them; whereas

Twice Beyond gives of himself into the worlds, and sows into them "*agile splendours*," as the Oracles phrase it (K., 16, 17). All this is a refinement of intellectual subtlety that need not detain us; it is foreign to the simpler mysticism of the Oracles.

THE GREAT MOTHER

Hecate is the Great Mother or Life of the universe, the Magna Mater, or Mother of the Gods and all creatures.

She is the Spouse of Mind, and simultaneously Mother and Spouse of Mind of Mind; she is, therefore, said to be centered between them.

K. 27.   *'Mid the Fathers the Centre of Hecate*
C. 65.   *circles.*

She is the Mother of souls, the Inbreather of life. Concerning this cosmic "vitalizing," or "quickening," or "ensouling" (psychosis), as Proclus calls it, three obscure verses are preserved:

K. 28.   *About the hollows beneath the ribs of*
          her right side there spouts, full-bursting,
C. 38.   *forth the Fountain of the Primal Soul,*
          all at once ensouling Light, Fire, Æther,
          Worlds.

If the "hollows beneath the ribs" is the correct translation (for the Greek seems very faulty, no matter what license we give to poetic imagery), it would appear that Hecate, the Great Mother, or World-Soul, was figured in woman's form. Hecate is, of course, as we have already remarked, not her native name (*nomen barbarum*), but the best equivalent the Greeks could find in their humanized pantheon, a bourgeois company as compared with the majestic, awesome and mysterious divinities of the Orient.

This was the cosmic *psychosis*; the mixture of individual souls was - acccording to the Trismegistic "Virgin of the World" treatise, and as we might naturally expect - of a somewhat more substantial, or plastic, nature. In this treatise we read:

"And since it neither thawed when fire was set to it (for it was made of Fire), nor yet did freeze when it had once been properly produced (for it was made of Breath), but kept its mixture's composition a certain special kind, peculiar to itself, of special type and special blend - (which composition you must know, God called *psychsis* . . .) - it was from this coagulate He fashioned souls enough in myriads" (H., iii. 99). It was probably in the mouth of the Great Mother that our poet placed the following lines:

K. 28.   *After the Father's Thinkings, you must*
C. 18.   *know, I, the Soul, dwell, making all*
            things to live by Heat.

In the mystery of re-generation also, as soon as the conception from the Father takes place - the implanting of the Light-spark, or germ of the spiritual man - the soul of the man becomes sensible to the passion of the Great Soul, the One and Only Soul, and he feels himself pulsing in the fiery net-work of lives.

But why, it may be asked, does the great Life-stream come forth from the Mother's right side? The fragments we possess do not tell us; but the original presumably contained some description of the Mother-Body, for we are told:

K. 28.   *On the left side of Hecate is a Fountain*
C. 187.   *of Virtue, remaining entirely within, not*
            sending forth its pure virginity.

39

We have thus to think out the symbolism in a far more vital mode than the figurative expressions naturally suggest. And again:

K. 29.   *And from her back, on either side the*
C. 141.   *Goddess, boundless Nature hangs.*

This suggests that Nature is the Garment or Mantle of the Goddess-Mother. The Byzantine commentators ascribe to every Limb of the Mother the power of life-giving; every Limb and Organ was a fountain of life. Her hair, her temples, the top of her head, her sides or flanks, were all so regarded; and even her dress, the coverings or veilings of her head, and her girdle. Whether they had full authority for this in the original text we do not know. Kroll considers this "*fraus aperta*" (K. 29); but the Mother of Life must be All-Life, one would have naturally thought, and one verse still preserved to us reads:

K. 29.   *Her hair seems like a Mane of Light*
C.128.   *a-bristle piercingly.*

Damascius speaks of her crown; this may possibly have been figured as the wall-crown or turreted diadem of Cybel' (Rhea), in which case it might have typified the "Walls of Fire" of Stoic tradition.

Her girdle seems to have been figured as a serpent of fire.

The Great Mother is also called Rhea in the Oracles, as the following three verses inform us:

K. 30.   *Rhea, in sooth, is both the Fountain*
            and the Flood of the blest Knowing
            Ones; for she it is who first receives the
C. 59.   *Father's Powers into her countless*

Bosoms, and poureth forth on every
thing birth [-and- death] that spins like
to a wheel.

The "Knowing Ones" are the Intelligences or Gnostic Thoughts of the Father. She is the Mother of Genesis, the Wheel or Sphere of Re-becoming. In one of her aspects she is called in the Oracles the "wondrous and awe-inspiring Goddess," as Proclus tells us. With the above verses may be compared K. 36, C. 140, 125 below.

ALL THINGS ARE TRIPLE

The statement of Hippolytus that the Assyrians (i.e., the Chaldæans) "were the first to consider the soul triple and yet one," is borne out by several quotations from our Oracle-poem.

K. 18. *The Mind of the Father uttered [the*
        Word] that all should be divided [or cut]
C. 28. *into three. His Will nodded assent, and*
        at once all things were so divided.

The Father-Mind thought "Three," acted "Three." Thought and action agreed, and it immediately happened.

An apparent continuation of this is found in the lines which characterize the Forth-thinker as:

K. 18. *He who governs all things with the Mind*
C. 29. *of the Eternal.*

This fundamental Triplicity of all things is "intelligible," that is to say, determined by the Mind. The Mind is the Great Measurer, Divider and Separator. Thus Philo of Alexandria writes concerning the Logos, or Mind or Reason of God:

"So God, having sharpened His Reason (Logos), the Divider of all things, cut off both the formless and undifferentiated essence of all things, and the four elements of cosmos which had been separated out of it [sci., the essence, or quintessence], and the animals and plants which had been compacted by means of these" (H., i. 236).

We learn from Damascius also that, according to our

Oracles, the "ideal division" (? of all things into three) was the "root (or source) of every division" in the sensible universe (K. 18, C. 58). This law was summed up as follows:

K. 18.   *In every cosmos there shineth [or is*
C. 36.   *manifested] a Triad, of which a Monad*
                  is source.

It is this Triad that "measures and delimits all things" (K. 18, C. 8) from highest to lowest. And again:

K. 18.   *All things are served in the Gulphs of*
C. 31.   *the Triad*

This is very obscure; but perhaps the following verse may throw some light on the imagery:

K. 18.   *From this Triad the Father mixed every*
C. 30.   *spirit.*

In the first verse "Gulphs" are generally translated by "Bosoms," and "are served" by "are governed"; but the latter expression is a technical Homeric term for serving the wine for libation purposes from the great mixing-bowl (krater) into the cups, and the mixing, or mingling or blending, of souls is operated, in Plato, in the great Mixing-bowl of the Creator. These gulphs are thus mother-vortices in primal space.

The "Three" is the number of determination, and therefore stands for the root-conditioning of form, and of all classification. But if the "Three" from one point of view is formative, and therefore determining and limiting, from another point of view, it endows with power; and so one of our Oracles runs:

K. 51.   *Arming both mind and soul with triple*
C. 170.   *Might.*

In the original, "triple" is a poetical term that might be rendered "three-barbed"; if, however, it is to be connected with Pythagoræan nomenclature, it would denote a triple angle - that is to say, presumably, the solid angle of a tetrahedron or regular four-faced pyramid.

THE MOTHER-DEPTHS

The Bosoms or Gulphs (? Vortices, Voragines, Whirl-swirls, Æons, Atoms) are also called Depths - a technical term of very frequent occurrence in all the Gnostic schools of the time. The Great Depth of all depths was that of the Father, the Paternal Depth. Thus one of our Oracles reads.

K. 18.   *Ye who, understanding, know the*
C. 168.   *Paternal Depth cosmos-transcending.*

This Paternal Depth is the ultimate mystery; but from another point of view it may be regarded as the Intelligible Ordering of all things. It is called super-cosmic or cosmos-transcending, when cosmos is regarded as the sensible or manifested order; it is the Occult, or Hidden, Eternal Type of universals, or wholes, simultaneously interpenetrating one another, undivided (sensibly) yet divided (intelligibly). We are told, therefore, concerning this super-cosmic or trans-mundane Depth, that

K. 19.   *It is all things, but intelligibly [all].*

That is to say, in it things are not divided in time and space; there is no sensible separation. It is not the specific state, or state of species; but the state of wholes or genera. It is neither Father nor Mother, yet both. It is the state of "At Once"; and perhaps this may explain the strange term "Once Beyond" - that is, the At-Once in the state of the Beyond, beyond the sensible divided cosmos. Proclus and Damascius speak of it as "of the form of oneness" and "indivisible"; and an Oracle characterizes it as:

> K. 19.   *That which cannot be cut up; the*
> *Holder-together of all sources.*

As such it may be regarded as the Mother-side of things, and thus is called:

> K. 19.   *Source of [all] sources, Womb that holds*
> C. 99.   *all things together.*

The Later Platonic commentators compared this with Plato's *Auto-zoon,* the 'Living Thing-in-itself', the Source of life to all; and thus the That-which-gives-life-to-itself; and, therefore, the Womb of all living creatures. The Oracles, however, regard it as the Womb of Life, the Divine Mother.

> K. 19.   *She is the Energizer [lit., Work-woman]*
> C. 55.   *and Forth-giver of Life-bringing Fire.*

"She fills the Life-giving Bosom [or Womb] of Hecate ." - the Supernal Mother's self-reflection in the sensible universe - says Proclus, basing himself on an Oracle, and:

> K. 19.   *Flows fresh and fresh [or on and on]*
> C. 55.   *into the wombs of things.*

The "wombs of things" are, literally, the "holders-together of things." They are reflections of the Great Holder-together of all sources" of the fourth fragment back. This poetical expression for the Mother-Depth and her infinite reflections in her own nature of manifoldness, was developed by the Later Platonic commentators into the formal designation of a hierarchy - the Synoches. That which she imparts is called:

K. 19.   *The Life-giving Might of Fire possessed of mighty power.*

This is all on the Mother-side of things; but this should never be divorced from the Father-side, as may be seen from the nature of the mysterious Æon.

THE ÆON

On the æon-doctrine (cf. H., i. 387-412), which probably occupied a prominent position in the mysticism of our Oracle-poem (though, of course, in a simple form and not as in the over-developed æonology of the Christianized Gnosis), we unfortunately possess only four verses.

One of the names given to the Æon was "*Father-begotten*" Light, because "He makes to shine His unifying light on all," as Proclus tells us.

K. 27.　　　*For He [the Æon] alone, culling unto its*
　　　　　　full the Flower of Mind [the Son] from
　　　　　　out the Father's Might [the Mother],
　　　　　　possesseth [both] the power to understand
C. 71.　　　*the Father's Mind, and to bestow that*
　　　　　　Mind both on all sources and upon all
　　　　　　principles, - both power to understand
　　　　　　[al., whirl], and ever bide upon His
　　　　　　never-tiring pivot.

The nature of this Æonic Principle (or } tmic Mystery), according to the belief of the Theurgists, is described by Proclus. But whether this description was based upon our poem or not, we cannot be certain. We, therefore, append what Proclus says, in illustration only (C. 2):

"Theurgists declare that He [Duration, Time without bounds, the Æon] is God, and hymn His divinity as both older [than old], and younger [than young], as ever-circling into itself [the Egg] and æon-wise; both as conceiving the sum total of all numbered things that move within the cosmos of His Mind, yet, over and beyond them all, as infinite by reason of His Power, and yet [again, when] viewed with them, as spirally convolved [the Serpent]."

The "ever-circling" is the principle of self-motivity. On the spiral-side of things there is procession to infinity; while on the sphere-side beginning and end are immediate and "at once."

With this passage must be taken two others quoted by Taylor, but without giving the references (C. 3 and 4):

"God [energizing] in the cosmos, æonian, boundless, young and old, in spiral mode convolved."

"For Eternity [the Æon], according to the Oracles, is Cause of Life that never falleth short, and of untiring Power, and restless Energy."

THE UTTERANCE OF THE FIRE

In connection with the idea of the Living Intellectual Fire as the Perfect Intelligible, Father and Mother in one (both creating Matter and impregnating it), conceived of sensibly as the "Descent into Matter," we may, perhaps, take the following verses:

K. 20.	*Thence there leaps forth the Genesis of Matter manifoldly wrought in varied*
C. 101.	*colours. Thence the Fire-flash down-streaming dims its [fair] Flower of Fire, as it leaps forth into the wombs of worlds.*
24.	*For thence all things begin downwards to shoot their admirable rays.*

The origin of matter and the genesis of matter is thus to be sought for in the Intelligible itself. The doctrine of the Pythagoræans and Platonists was that the origin of matter was to be traced to the Monad. The Flower of Fire is here the quintessence of it.

LIMIT THE SEPARATOR

To the same part of the poem we must also refer the following:

K. 20.   *For from Him leap forth both Thunderings*
          inexorable, and the Fireflash-receiving
          Bosoms of the All-fiery Radiance of
C. 66.   *Father-begotten Hecate , and that by which*
          the Flower of Fire and mighty Breath
          beyond the fiery poles is girt.

Those who have studied attentively the *Mithriac Ritual* (Vol. VI.), will feel themselves in a familiar atmosphere when reading these lines. The "Thunderings" are the Creative Utterances of the Father; the "Bosoms" of Hecate are the receptive vortices on the Mother-side of things. Yet Father and Mother and also Son are all three the Monad. She is "Father-begotten - the Monad perpetually giving birth to itself. The Son is the that which "girds" or limits or separates, the Gnostic Horos or Limit, the Form-side of things, which shuts out the Below from the Above, and determines all opposites. It is the Cross, the "Undergirding" of the universe, as we have seen in *The Gnostic Crucifixion* (Vol. VII., pp. 15, 43 ff.).

The commentators, however, with their rage for intellectual precision, have turned this into a technical term, making it a special name; but in the Oracles *hypezokos* is used more simply and generally as the separator.

Proclus characterizes this as the prototype of division, the "separation of the things-that-are from matter," basing himself apparently on the verse:

K. 22.   *Just as a diaphragm, (hypezokos) a*
          knowing membrane, He divides.

The nature of this separation is that of "knowing" or "gnostic" Fire. The Epicuræans called the separation between the visible and invisible the "Flaming Walls" of the universe. Compare the Angel with the flaming sword who guards the Gates of Paradise.

So also with the epithet "inexorable" (*ameíliktoi*) applied to the "Thunderings"; these have been transformed by the over-elaboration of the commentators into a hierarchy of Inexorables or Implacables, just as is the gorgeous imagery of the Coptic Gnostic treatises of the Askew and Bruce codices.

The simpler use may be seen in the following two verses:

K. 21.   *The Mind of the Father, vehicled in rare*
          Drawers-of-straight-lines, flashing
          inflexibly in furrows of implacable Fire.
C. 17.

This seems to refer to the Rays of the Divine Intelligence vehicled in creative Fire. It is the Divine Ploughing of primal substance. Straight lines are characteristic of the Mind.

It is the first furrowing, so to speak, of the Sea of Matter in a universal pattern that impresses upon the surface a network of Light (as may be seen in protoplasm under a strong microscope) from the Ruler of the Sea above. It is the first Descent of the Father, and the first Ascent or Arising of the Son; it suggests the idea of riding and controlling. The epithet "rare" or "attenuated" suggests drawn out to the finest thread; these threads or lines govern and map out the Sea; they are the Lines on the Surface; they glitter and look like furrows of the essence of Fire.

THE EMANATION OF IDEAS

In close connection with the lines beginning "For from Him leap forth," we may take the longest fragment (16 lines) preserved to us:

K. 23.

The Father's Mind forth-bubbled,
conceiving, with His Will in all its prime,
Ideas that can take upon themselves all
forms; and from One Source they,

C. 39.

taking flight, sprang forth. For from the
Father was both Will and End.
These were made differentiate by
Gnostic Fire, allotted into different
knowing modes.
For, for the world of many forms, the
King laid out an intellectual Plan [or
Type] not subject unto change. Kept to
the tracing of this Plan, that no world
can express, the World, made glad with
the Ideas that take all shapes, grew
manifest with form.
Of these Ideas there is One only Source,
from which there bubble-forth in
differentiation other [ones] that no one
can approach - forth-bursting round
the bodies of the World - which circle
round its awe-inspiring Depths [or
Bosoms], like unto swarms of bees,
flashing around them and about,

incuriously, some hither and some
thither, - the Gnostic Thoughts from the
Paternal Source that cull unto their full
the Flower of Fire at height of sleepless
Time.
It was the Father's first self-perfect
Source that welled-forth these original Ideas.

With this "culling" or "plucking" of the Flower of Fire compare the ancient gnomic couplet preserved by Hesiod (O. et D., 741 f.):

"Nor from Five-branched at Gods' Fire-looming
Cut Dry from Green with flashing Blade."

As has been previously stated (H., i. 265, n. 5), I believe that Hesiod has preserved this scrap of ancient wisdom from the "Orphic" fragments in circulation in his day among the people in Bœotia, who had them from an older Greece than that of Homer's heroes; in other words, that we have in it a trace of the contact of pre-Homeric Greece with "Chaldæa."

These living Ideas or creative Thoughts are emanations (or forth-flowings) of the Divine Mind, and constitute the Plan of that Mind, the Divine Economy. They are more transcendent even than the Fire, for they are said to be able to gather for themselves the subtlest essence or Flower of Fire. "At height of sleepless Time" is a beautiful phrase, though it is difficult to assign to it a very precise meaning. The "height of Time" is, perhaps, the supreme moment, and thus may mean momentarily - not, however, in the sense of lasting only the smallest fraction of time, but referring to Time at its limit where it touches Eternity.

The Thoughts of the Father-Mind are on the Borderland of Time. They are living Intelligences of Light and Life, of the nature of Logoi.

K. 24.   *Thoughts of the Father! Brightness*
              a-flame, pure Fire!

THE BOND OF LOVE DIVINE

Next we may take the verses referring to the Birth of Love (Eros), the Bond-of-union between all things.

K. 25.   *For the Self-begotten One, the Father-*
            Mind, perceiving His [own] Works,
            sowed   into all Love's Bond, that with
            his Fire o'ermasters all; so that all
C. 107.   *might continue loving on for endless*
            time, and that these Weavings of the
            Father's Gnostic Light might never fail.
            With this Love, too, it is the Elements of
            Cosmos keep on running.

The Works of the Father are the Operations of the Divine Mind - the Souls. The same idea, though on a lower scale, so to say, may be seen in the Announcement of the Monarch of the Worlds, sitting on the Throne of Truth, to the Souls, in the Trismegistic "Virgin of the World" treatise:

"O Souls, Love and Necessity shall be your Lords, they who are Lords and Marshals after Me of all" (H., ii. 110).

The Marriage of the Elements and their perpetual transmutation was one of the leading doctrines of Heraclitus. The Elements married and transformed themselves into one another, as may also be seen from the Magian myth quoted in Vol. V. of these little books, *The Mysteries of Mithra* (pp. 49-52). The idea is summed up in the following fine lines from a Hymn of Praise to the Æon or Eternity, in the Magic Papyri:

"Hail unto Thee, O Thou Beginning and Thou End of Nature naught can move! Hail unto Thee, Thou Vortex of the Liturgy [or Service] unweariable of Nature's Elements!"

In close connection with the above verses of our poem we must plainly take the following:

K. 25.   *With the Bond of admirable Love, who*
C. 23.   *leaped forth first, clothed round with*
           Fire, his fellow bound to him, that he
           might mix the Mixing-bowls original by
           pouring in the Flower of his own Fire.

In the last line I read picîn ("pouring in") for piscèn. The Mixing-bowls, or Krateres, are the Fiery Crucibles in which the elements and souls of things are mixed. The Mixer is not Love as apart from the Father, but the Mind of the Father as Love, as we learn from the following verses:

K. 26.   *Having mingled the Spark of Soul with*
           two in unanimity - with Mind and Breath
           Divine - to them He added, as a third,
C. 81.   *pure Love, the august Master binding all.*

Compare with this the Mixing of Souls in "The Virgin of the World" treatise:

"For taking breath from His own Breath and blending with it Knowing Fire, He mingled them with other substances which have no power to know; and having made the two - either with other - one, with certain hidden Words of Power, He thus set all the mixture going thoroughly" (H., iii. 98).

This Chaste and Holy and Divine Love is invoked as follows in the Paris Papyrus (1748):

"Thee I invoke, Thou Primal Author of all generation, who dost out-stretch Thy wings o'er all the universe; Thee the unapproachable, Thee the immeasurable, who dost inspire into all souls the generative sense [lit., reason], who dost conjoin all things by power of Thine own Self" (K. 26).

Elsewhere in the same Papyrus (1762), Love is called:

"The Hidden One who secretly doth cause to spread among all souls the Fire that cannot be attained by contemplation."

What men think of as love, is, as contrasted with this Divine Love, called in our Oracles, the "stifling of True Love." True Love is also called "Deep Love," with which we are to fill our souls, as Proclus tells us (K. 26). Elsewhere in the Oracles this Love was united with Faith and Truth into a triad, which may be compared with another triad in the following verse quoted by Damascius:

K. 27.   *Virtue and Wisdom and deliberate*
              Certainty.
C. 35.

So far we have been dealing with the Divine Powers when conceived as transcending the manifested universe; we now come to the world-shaping, or economy of the material cosmos, and to the Powers concerned with it.

THE SEVEN FIRMAMENTS

As we have seen above, in treating of the Great Mother (p. 46), it is she who, as the Primal Soul, "all at once ensouls Light, Fire, Æther, Worlds" (K. 28, C. 38).

The Later Platonist commentators regard this Light as a monad embracing a triad of states - empyrean, ætherial, and hylic (that is, of gross matter). They further assert that the last state only is visible to normal physical sight (K. 31).

These four thus constituted the quaternary or tetrad of the whole sensible universe. This would, of course, be somewhat of a daring "philosophizing" of the simple statement of the original poem, if the verse we have quoted were the only authority for the precise statement of the commentators. But we are hardly justified in assuming, as Kroll appears to do throughout, that if no verse is quoted, therefore no verse existed. The Platonic commentators had the full poem before them, and (like the systematizers of the Upanishads) tried to evolve a consistent system out of its mystic utterances. There were also, in the highest probability, other Hellenistic documents of a similar character, giving back some reflections from the "Books of the Chaldæans"; and also in the air a kind of general tradition of a "Chaldæan philosophy."

The Sensible Universe was thus divided by them, basing themselves on the pregnant imagery of the Oracles, into three states or "planes" - the empyrean, ætherial, and hylic. To these planes or states they referred the mysterious septenary of spheres mentioned in the verse:

K. 31.

> *The Father caused to swell forth seven*
> *firmaments of worlds.*

C. 120.

This Father is, of course, Mind of Mind, and the "causing to swell forth" gives the idea of the swelling from a centre to the limit of a surround.

The most interesting point is that those who knew the Oracles, and were in the direct line of their tradition, did not regard these seven firmaments or zones as the "planetary orbits." One of the seven they assigned to the empyrean, three to the ætherial, and three to the gross-material or sublunary. There was thus a chain or coil of seven depending from the eighth, the octave, of Light, the Borderland between the intelligible and the sensible worlds. All the seven, however, were "corporeal" worlds (K. 32). The three hylic (those of gross matter) may be compared with the solid, liquid and gaseous states of physical matter; the three ætherial with similar states of æther or subtle matter; and the seventh corresponds with the atomic or empyrean or true fiery or fire-mist state.

Moreover, as to the hylic world or world of gross matter, which had three spheres or states, we learn:

K. 33.   *The centres of the hylic world are fixed*
          in the æther above it.

That is to say, presumably, the æther was supposed to surround and interpenetrate the cosmos of gross matter.

THE TRUE SUN

As to the Sun, the tradition handed on a mysterious doctrine that cannot now be completely recovered in the absence of the original text. Proclus, however, tell us that the real Sun, as distinguished from the visible disk, was trans-mundane or super-cosmic - that is, beyond the worlds visible to the senses. In other words, it belonged to the Light-world proper, the monadic cosmos, and poured forth thence its "fountains of Light." The tradition of the most arcane or mystic of the Oracles, he tells us, was that the Sun's "wholeness" - i.e., monad - was to be sought on the trans-mundane plane (K. 32, C. 130); "for there," he says, "is the '*Solar Cosmos*' and the '*Whole Light,*' as the Oracles of the Chaldæans say, and I believe" (K. 33).

Elsewhere he speaks of "what appears to be the circuit of the Sun," and contrasts this with its true circulation, "which, proceeding from above somewhere, from out the hidden and super-celestial ordering of things beyond the heavens, sows into all the (suns) in cosmos the proper portion of their light for each." This also seems to have been based on the doctrine of the Oracles.

As the Enforming Mind was called Mind of Mind, so was the "truer Sun" called in the Oracles "*Time of Time*," because it measures all things with Time, as Proclus tells us; and this Time is, of course, the Æon. It was also called "*Fire, Sluice of Fire,*" and also "*Fire-disposer*" (K. 33, C. 133), and, we may add, by many another name connected with Fire, as we learn from the *Mithriac Ritual*.

THE MOON

If the visible sun, as we have seen, was not the true Sun, equally so must we suppose the visible moon to be an image of the true Moon reflected in the atmosphere of gross matter. Concerning the Moon we have these five scattered shreds of fragments.

K. 33.	*Both the ætherial course and the measureless rush and the a' rial floods [or fluxes] of the Moon.*
C. 135.	
K. 33.	*O Æther, Sun, Moon's Breath, Leaders of Air!*
C. 136.	
K. 33.	*Both of the solar circles and lunar pulsings and aerial bosoms.*
C.139.	
K. 33.	*The melody of Æther and of Sun, and of the streams of Moon and Air.*
C. 139.	
K. 34.	*And wide Air, and lunar course, and the ætherial vault of Sun.*
C. 137.	

These scraps are too fragmentary to comment on with much profit.

THE ELEMENTS

From what remains we learn, as Proclus tells us, that the Sun-space came first, then the Moon-space, and then the Air-space. The Elements of cosmos, however, were not simply our Earthy fire, air, water, and earth, but of a greater order. Thus Olympiodorus tells us that the elements at the highest points of the earth, that is on the tops of the highest mountains, were also thought of as elements of cosmic Water - as it were Watery air; and this air in its turn was (? moist) Æther, while Æther itself was the uttermost Æther; it was in that state that were to be sought the "*Æthers of the Elements*" proper, as the Oracles call them (K. 34, C. 112).

THE SHELLS OF THE COSMIC EGG

The diagrammatic representation of cosmic limit was a curve; whether hyperbolic, parabolic or elliptical we do not know. Damascius, quoting from the Oracles, speaks of it as a single line - "*drawn out in a curved (or convex) outline,*" or figure; and adds that this figure was frequently used in the Oracles (K. 34). It signified the periphery of heaven.

In the Orphic mythology (doubtless based on "Chaldæan" sources) the dome of heaven is fabled to have been formed out of the upper shell of the Great Egg, when it broke in twain. The Egg in its upper half was sphere-like, in its lower "conical" or elliptical.

Proclus tells us that the Oracles taught that there were seven circuits or rounds of the irregular or imperfect "spheres," and in addition the single motion of the eighth or perfect sphere which carried the whole heaven round in the contrary direction towards the west.

THE PHYSIOLOGY OF THE
COSMIC BODY

To this eighth sphere we must refer the "progression," spoken of in the verses:

K. 34.   *Both lunar course and star-progression.*
            [This] star-progression was not delivered
            from the womb of things because of thee.
C. 144.

Man, the normal mind of man, was subject to the irregular spheres; he is egg-shaped and not spherical. And if there were spheres there were also certain mysterious "centres," and "channels" - pipes, canals, conduits, or ducts; but what and how many these were, we can no longer discover owing to the loss of the original text. One obscure fragment alone remains:

K. 35.   *And fifth, [and] in the midst, another*
            fiery sluice, whence the life-bringing
            Fire descendeth to the hylic channels.
C. 92.

This apparently concerns the anatomy and physiology of the Great Body. Proclus introduces this quotation with the statement: "The conduit of the Power-of-generating-lives descends into the centre [of the cosmos], as also the Oracles say, when discoursing on the middle one of the five centres that extends right through to the opposite [side], through the centre of the earth."

How a centre can enter and go through another centre is not clear. These channels or centres, however, were clearly ways of conveying the nourishing and sustaining Fire to the world and all the lives in it.

The Primal Centre of the universe is presumably referred to in the following verse:

K. 65.   *The Centre, from which all [? rays] to*
           the periphery are equal.

C. 124.

THE GLOBULAR COSMOS

In any case the root-plan of the universe was globular. Proclus tells us that God as the Demiurge, or World-shaper, made the whole cosmos:

K. 35.   *From Fire, from Water, Earth, and all-*
              nourishing Æther.
C. 118.

Where Æther is presumably the "Watery Æther" or Air, as we have seen above (p. 80). He tells us further that the Maker, working by Himself, or on Himself, or with His own Hands, framed, or shaped (*lit.*, "carpentered") the cosmos, as follows:

K. 35.   *Yea, for there was a Second Mass of Fire*
              working of its own self all things
C. 108.   *below (lit., there), in order that the*
              Cosmic Body might be wound into
              a ball, in order that Cosmos might be
              made plainly manifest, and not appear
              as membrane-like.

It is, of course, very difficult to guess the meaning of these scraps without their context. The appearance of cosmos as membranous, however, suggests the idea of the thinnest skin or surface, that is the lines, or threads, or initial markings, on the surface of things; that is to say, that the action of the Enforming Fire rolls up the surfaces of things into three-dimensional things or solids (even as the threads of wool are wound into a ball). The underlying idea may be seen in another Oracle, which referring to the Path of Return, where the mode of Outgoing, or Involving, has to be reversed or unwound, warns us:

K. 64.   *Do not soil the spirit, nor turn the plane*
          into the solid.
C. 152.

To this we shall return later on at the end of our comments. (Cf. H., iii. 174).

The "Second Mass of Fire" is, presumably, the Sensible Fire, or rather the Fire that brings into manifestation the sensible world, as contrasted with the Pure Hidden Fire - the Unmanifest, Intelligible or Ideal Mind of the Father. The Second is of course Mind of Mind, poetically figured, as contrasted with Mind in itself; it is Mind going forth from itself.

The word translated "Mass" (*Ôgkoj*) has a variety of refined meanings in Greek philosophical language; it can mean space, dimension, atom, etc., and gives the idea of the simplest determination of Body.

The World or Cosmos is, so to say, the "Outline" of the Mind turned to the thought of Body:

K. 35.   *For it is a Copy of Mind; but that which*
          is brought forth [or engendered] has
          something of Body.
C. 110.

The whole of Nature, of growth and evolution, depends or derives its origin, from the Great Mother, the Spouse of Deity, as we have seen from the verse quoted above (p. 49, K. 29, C. 141). In some way Nature is identified with Fate and Custom, as the following three verses show.

K. 36.   *For Nature that doth never tire, rules*
          over worlds and works; in order that the
C. 140.   *Heaven may run its course for aye,*
          down-drawn, and the swift Sun, around
          its Centre, that custom-wise he may
          return.

125.

If by Apollo Proclus means the Sun, and if "one of the
Theurgists" is a reference to the writer of our poem, then the
words "*exulting in the Harmony of Light*" may be compared
with the familiar "rejoicing as a giant to run his course." The
Oracles speak of the Sun as possessing "*three-powered* (lit.,
three-winged) rule" - that is, presumably, above, on, and
beneath the earth.

THE PRINCIPLES OR RULERS OF
THE SENSIBLE WORLD

In the fragments that remain it is very rare to find the Powers that administer the government of the universe, given Greek names. Though Proclus refers the following verse to Athʻ na, there is nothing to show that her name was mentioned in the Oracles. It is more probable (as we may see from K. 51, C. 170, below) that the phrase refers to the soul, or rather the new-born man of gnostic power, who leaps forth from his lower nature. Proclus may have seen in this an analogy with the birth of Athʻ na full-armed from the head of Zeus, and so the confusion has arisen. The phrase runs:

K. 36.   *Yea, verily, full-armed within and armed*
            without, like to a goddess.
C. 171.

The first epithet is used of the Trojan Horse with the armed warriors within it. In the mystery of re-generation this may refer to the re-making of all man's "bodies" according to the cut and pattern of the Great or Cosmic Body. This would be all on the Mother-side of things - the gestation of the true Body of Resurrection.

It is the Later Platonic commentators, most probably, who have added names from the Hellenic pantheon in elaborating the simple, and for the most part nameless, statements of the original poem.

It is, however, clear that corresponding with what are

called Fountains when considered as Sources of Light and Life, in the Intelligible, there were Principles, Rulerships or Sovereignties, which ruled and ordered the Sensible Cosmos.

That these were divided into a hierarchy of four triads, twelve in all, as our commentators would have it, matches, it is true, with the Twelve of the traditional Chaldæan star-lore; but this was probably not so definitely set forth in the original text. Concerning these Principles the following lines are preserved:

K. 37.

> *Principles which, perceiving in their*
> *minds the Works thought in the*

C. 73.

> *Father's Mind, clothed them about with*
> *works and bodies that the sense can*
> *apprehend.*

The chief ruling Principles of the sensible world were three in number. Damascius calls them "the three Fathers" - *sci.*, of the manifested cosmos; but this seems to be an echo of the nomenclature of the Theurgic or Magical school and not of the Oracles proper. He, however, quotes the following three verses with regard to the threefold division of the sensible world.

K. 37.

> *Among them the first Course is the*
> *Sacred one; and in the midst the Aëry;*
> *third is another [one] which warms the*

C. 37.

> *Earth in Fire. For all things are the*
> *slaves of these three mighty Principles.*

This seems to mean, according to Damascius, that corresponding with the Heaven, Earth, and the Interspace, Air, there are three Principles; or rather, there is One Principle in three modes - heavenly (or empyrean), middle (aëry or ætherial), and terrene (or hylic). The heavenly course is, presumably, the revolution of the Great Sphere of fixed stars; the terrene is connected with the Central Fire; and the middle with the motions of the irregular spheres.

It may also be that the last "course," connected with the Air simply, has to do with the mysterious "Winds" or currents of the Great Breath, as we saw in the symbolism of the *Mithriac Ritual*. This conjecture is confirmed by certain obscure references in Damascius, when, using the language of the Oracles, he speaks of a "*Pipe*" or "*Conduit*" connected with the Principles of the sensible world, and says that this is subordinate to a Pipe connected with the Fountains of the intelligible world.

The difference between Fountain and Principle is clear enough; one wells out from itself, the other rules something not itself. The terms seem to be somewhat of a *hysteron proteron* if we insist on a precise meaning; we should remember, however, that we are dealing largely with symbolism and poetical imagery.

Proclus endeavours to draw up a precise scale of terms in connection with this imagery of Fountains or Sources, when he tells us that the highest point of every chain (or series) is called a Fountain (or Source); next came Springs; after these Channels; and then Streams. But this is probably a refinement of Proclus' and not native to the Logia.

Finis

Parchment Books is committed to publishing high quality Esoteric/Mystic classic texts at a reasonable price.

With the premium on space in modern dwellings, we also strive - within the limits of good book design - to make our products as slender as possible, allowing more books to be fitted into a given bookshelf area.

Parchment Books is an imprint of Aziloth Books, which has established itself as a publisher boasting a diverse list of powerful, quality titles, including novels of flair and originality, and factual publications on controversial issues that have not found a home in the rather staid and politically-correct atmosphere of many publishing houses.

Titles Include:

Secret Doctrines of the Rosicrucians	Magus Incognito
Corpus Hermeticum	GRS Mead (trans.)
The Virgin of the World	Hermes Trismegistus
Raja Yoga	Yogi Ramacharaka
Knowledge of the Higher Worlds and Its Attainment	Steiner
Conference of the Birds	Farid ud-Din Attar
The Gospel of Thomas	Anonymous
Pistis Sophia	GRS Mead (trans.)
The Secret Destiny of America	Manly P Hall
Heretics	G K Chesterton

Obtainable at all good online and local bookstores.
View Parchment Book's full list at:
www.azilothbooks.com

We are a small, approachable company and would love to hear any of your comments and suggestions on our plans, products, or indeed on absolutely anything. Aziloth is also interested in hearing from aspiring authors whom we might publish. We look forward to meeting you.

Contact us at: info@azilothbooks.com

CATHEDRAL CLASSICS

Parchment Book's sister imprint, Cathedral Classics, hosts an array of classic literature, from ancient tomes to twentieth-century masterpieces, all of which deserve a place in your home. A small selection is detailed below:

Mary Shelley	*Frankenstein*
H G Wells	*The Time Machine; The Invisible Man*
Niccolo Machiavelli	*The Prince*
Omar Khayyam	*The Rubaiyat of Omar Khayyam*
Joseph Conrad	*Heart of Darkness; The Secret Agent*
Jane Austen	*Persuasion; Northanger Abbey*
Oscar Wilde	*The Picture of Dorian Gray*
Voltaire	*Candide*
Bulwer Lytton	*The Coming Race*
Arthur Conan Doyle	*The Adventures of Sherlock Holmes*
John Buchan	*The Thirty-Nine Steps*
Friedrich Nietzsche	*Beyond Good and Evil*
Henry James	*Washington Square*
Stephen Crane	*The Red Badge of Courage*
Ralph Waldo Emmerson	*Self-Reliance, & Other Essays (series1&2)*
Sun Tzu	*The Art of War*
Charles Dickens	*A Christmas Carol*
Fyodor Dostoyevsky	*The Gambler; The Double*
Virginia Wolf	*To the Lighthouse; Mrs Dalloway*
Johann W Goethe	*The Sorrows of Young Werther*
Walt Whitman	*Leaves of Grass - 1855 edition*
Confucius	*Analects*
Anonymous	*Beowulf*
Anne Bronte	*Agnes Grey*
More	*Utopia*

full list at: www.azilothbooks.com
Obtainable at all good online and local bookstores.

THE CARTON CHRONICLES

THE CURIOUS TALE OF FLASHMAN'S TRUE FATHER

Keith Laidler

Morose, cynical and given to drink, Sydney Carton is one of Charles Dickens' most famous characters; a cold, dispassionate man, yet capable, in the final moments of A Tale of Two Cities, of sacrificing himself beneath the guillotine for Lucie, the woman he both loved and lost.

It now appears, however, that Dickens was being somewhat economical with the *actualité*.

Newly recovered documents, written in Carton's own hand, tell a far different tale. Sydney Carton survived his execution, only to find himself at the mercy of the monstrous Robespierre, author of the Paris Terror. His love Lucie languishes in a French prison, her husband dead, and Carton can ensure her survival only by becoming Robespierre's personal spy.

Reluctant, terrified and often drunk, Carton blunders his way through the major events of the French Revolution, grudgingly partaking in some of the blackest deeds of the Terror and, by a mixture of cowardice, bravado and luck, lending a hand in the fall of most of its leading figures. Kidnapped by the British, he finds himself a double agent, trusted by neither side. Our hero chronicles the slow decay of revolutionary ideals and, in passing, casts light on the true parentage of that sadistic villain of "Tom Brown's Schooldays", the beastly Flashman.

Praise for Keith Laidler's writing:

"Laidler's book is meticulously researched and covers a fascinating period" (The Times)

"It is a riveting story, and Laidler tells it well" (Sunday Telegraph Review)

From all good online and local bookstores.

Milton Keynes UK
Ingram Content Group UK Ltd.
UKHW021611050624
443649UK00016BA/827